PREFACE

Japanese food is becoming popular in the United States, other countries, as well as in Asian countries. Once you acquire the delicate taste of it, you will savor the fine art of Japanese cuisine. Furthermore, it is considered an excellent health food, low in calories and nutritionally well balanced. By chance, if you are one of those who have not been exposed to fish, especially raw fish, and tend to stay away from it, you should not hesitate to try fresh fish prepared the Japanese way. You will be surprised to find out how simple, delicious, and satisfying it is.

Japanese food is unique in flavor, color, and appearance. By using simple mild seasonings, the natural flavor of the ingredients is retained, creating an exquisite aroma, very exciting and very inviting. Traditional creative arrangements of the food for color and appearance is an art itself and make the selections more appetizing.

Basic techniques such as cutting, soup stock (*dashi* 出し) preparation, fish filleting, and fillet-slicing methods as well as pickling (漬け物) and various sauce preparations are presented under Techniques of Japanese Cooking. Furthermore, ten lessons have been carefully selected to introduce essential techniques which cover most Japanese food preparations. Each lesson is treated individually with detailed instructions, shown step-by-step with easy to follow color photos.

Beginning with the simple soup, *miso shiru* (*shirumono*, 汁物), the following lessons are presented: clear soup (*suimono* 吸い物); salad (*sunomono* 酢の物); steamed food, *chawan mushi* (*mushimono* 蒸し物); noodle dish, *udon* (*menrui* めん類); grilled dish, *teriyaki* (*yakimono* 焼き物); deep-fried dish, *tempura* (*agemono* 揚げ物); one-pot dish, *sukiyaki* (*nabemono* 鍋物); raw fish preparation (*sashimi* 刺し身); and three varieties of *sushi* (すし) such as *nigiri-zushi* (にぎりずし), *nori-maki* (のり巻), *gunkan-maki* (軍艦巻).

For newcomers to Japanese cooking, this book will provide an excellent opportunity to learn Japanese cooking at home and at your own pace — the most effective way to learn. Those who are already familiar with Japanese cooking will be able to move up the ladder and become great chefs of Japanese cuisine.

Florence C. Lee
Helen C. Lee

TABLE OF CONTENTS

I. INGREDIENTS

VEGETABLES, NOODLES AND OTHER ESSENTIALS

1. Anchovies (dried) — Used for soup stock.
2. Bamboo shoots — Fibrous with a crunchy texture; have a subtle, mild taste and flavor.
3. Bean curd, fresh (*tofu*)— Made from soy beans and is rich in protein; quite soft and should be handled carefully.
4. Bean curd, fried (*aburahage*) — Deep fried bean curd.
5. Bonito shavings (*katsuobushi*) — Bonito meat cooked, dried, and shaved into flakes; used for soup stock.
6. Burdock roots — Long, slender roots; have a crunchy texture and a mild flavor.
7. Celery cabbage — A stocky oblong shape with rounded leaves on thick stalks.
8. Chrysanthemum leaves, edible — Tender and refreshing aromatic leaves; used in salad, clear soups, and one pot dishes.
9. Devil's tongue jelly (*konnyaku*) — Made from the starch of *Amorphophalus konjac* root;

available in dense, gelatinous cakes, hazy brown to gray.

10. Fish cake (*kamaboko*) — The meat of white-fleshed fish cooked, mashed, seasoned, and steamed in molds; widely used in noodle dishes and soups.

11. Fish *oboro* — The meat of white-fleshed fish cooked, mashed and seasoned, then, dried and granulated; used in rolled *sushi*.

12. Fish roe — Used as filling for *gungan-maki* (battleship-shaped *sushi*).

13. Gourd, dried (*kampyo*) — Japanese gourd pith shaved and dried, comes in long strips; used as filling for rolled *sushi*.

14. Green onions — Widely used in seasoning sauces, soups, and noodle dishes; lend an aromatic flavor to the food as well as an appetizingly fresh color to the dish.

15. Japanese mushrooms (*shiitake* mushrooms), fresh — Used for its aroma, appearance, and texture.

16. Japanese mushrooms (*shiitake* mushrooms), dried — Its flavor is slightly different from that of fresh mushrooms, but it is still very aromatic.

17. Japanese vermicelli (*shirataki*) — Thin transparent gelatinous noodles made from tuber root starch.

18. Kelp (*kombu*)— Dried strips of seaweed; used for soup stock and in other recipes for its subtle flavor.

19. Kelp, seasoned (*oboro kombu*) — *Kombu* leaves soaked in vinegar and shaved cross-wise. Comes in sheets; used in soups, noddle dishes, salad, and rice balls (*nigiri*).

20. Lotus roots — Thick cream colored rhizomes with tubular hollows give attractive flower-like patterns when cut into rounds.

21. *Mugi* noodles — Barley noodles; usually served cold.

22. *Nori* seaweed — Thin sheets of seaweed; used in making rolled *sushi*.

23. Radish, Japanese (*daikon*) — Long and thick white radish; used in salad, steamed dishes, and dipping sauces (also pickled).

24. Rice — Short-grain rice has a chewy texture and clings together nicely. It is preferred by all rice lovers.

25. Shrimp, small (dried) — Used for soup stock.

26. *Soba* noodles — Buckwheat noodles; served hot or cold.

27. *Somen* noodles — Thin wheat noodles; served hot or cold.

28. *Udon* noodles — Quite thick wheat noodles; usually served hot.

SPICES AND SEASONINGS

29. Corn Starch
30. Ginger
31. *Mirin* (sweetened rice wine)
32. *Miso* (fermented soy bean paste)
33. Rice vinegar
34. Sesame seeds
35. Sherry
36. Soy sauce, light
37. Soy sauce, dark
38. Sugar
39. *Teri* sauce
40. *Wasabi* (Japanese green mustard)

II. TECHNIQUES OF JAPANESE COOKING

USE OF CHOPSTICKS

Chopsticks are the principal eating utensils in China, Japan, Korea, and several other Asian countries. They are also useful in the kitchen for mixing, whipping, stirring, and picking up food.

They come in various sizes and shapes and are made of different materials. One can find elaborate chopsticks made of enameled wood, ivory, bone, or even silver and gold. However, chopsticks used in cooking are usually made of wood or bamboo and are 10 to 12 inches long.

1 Hold one chopstick between the tips of the thumb and the index finger and rest it on the side of the middle finger, as you would hold a pencil — about two-thirds up the length of the chopstick. Practice moving the chopstick back and forth with the index and middle fingers while the thumb remains still.

2 Insert the second chopstick between the base of the thumb and the fourth finger, resting against the nail.

3 Pick up a piece of food by bringing the tip of the top chopstick to the tip of the bottom one: move only the top chopstick with the index and middle fingers. Do not move the bottom one.

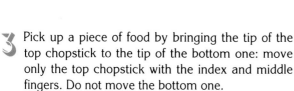

CUTTING TECHNIQUES

ROUND SLICES, HALF-MOON SLICES, AND QUARTER SLICES

Round Slices

1. Hold the vegetable — here, the radish — with your left hand (if right-handed) and curve in your finger tips, knuckles guiding the blade of the knife. Insert the blade of the knife perpendicular to the radish.

2. Cut the radish straight down at about 1/8 to 1/4-inch (3 to 6-mm) intervals. The thickness of the cut pieces is regulated by the distance the fingers move after each cutting.

Half-moon Slices

Cut the round pieces in half. Or, you may halve the radish lengthwise, then cut the halved blocks crosswise at 1/8 to 1/4-inch (3 to 6-mm) intervals or at any even intervals as desired.

Quarter Slices

Cut the half-moon slices in half. Or, you may quarter the radish lengthwise, then slice the quartered pieces crosswise at 1/8 to 1/4-inch (3 to 6-mm) intervals.

SLANT CUTTING AND STRAIGHT CUTTING

Slant Cutting

Place the blade at a 30 to 45 degree angle to the food — here, the green onions — holding it from the side with your left hand. Curve in the finger tips, knuckles serving as a guide for the blade. Move the hand to the left after each cutting motion of the knife. The thickness of the cut pieces is regulated by the distance the fingers move.

Straight Cutting

Hold the food — here, the green onions— perpendicular to the blade of the knife with your left hand. Cut straight into the food.

11

OBLIQUE CUTTING (WEDGE CUTTING)

Oblique cutting creates three exposed surfaces, so that the cut pieces are able to absorb the seasoning better and cook faster. Burdock roots, carrots, and radishes are often times cut in oblique shapes.

1 Slant cut the vegetable — here, the carrot.

2 Turn it toward you with your left hand until the cut-surface is facing directly upward.

3 Make another slant-cut. Repeat this turn-and-cut steps. The size of the cut pieces depends on the angle of the knife inserted to the food.

SHAVINGS

1 Hold the vegetable — here, the burdock root — with your left hand and insert the blade of the knife as if in a pencil sharpening motion, cutting the root into long and thin pieces. The angle of the blade to the food determines the thickness of the cut pieces.

2 Rotate the root and repeat cutting.

* The cut pieces of the burdock root should be immersed immediately in water or in an acidic solution (1 teaspoon of vinegar or lemon juice in one pint of water) to prevent them from turning brown and also to remove bitterness.

CUBES

1 Slice the food— here, the bean curd, ½ block, 2 × 4 × 1½-inch (5 × 10 × 3.8-cm) — into three pieces, ½-inch (1.3-cm) thick.

2 Cut the pieces lengthwise into three strips.

3 Cut the strips into ½-inch (1.3-cm) cubes.

HAIRY STRIPS

Hairy strips of radish are used as beds for *sashimi*.

1. Cut the vegetable — here, the Japanese radish — crosswise at about 2-inch (5-cm) intervals.

2. Hold the round side of the radish block with your left hand, placing the thumb in the middle of the side of the radish.

3. Now, insert the blade of the knife almost parallel to the radish, with the right thumb close to the edge of the blade and the index finger on the back of the blade, guiding the cutting.

4. Move the knife in a rhythmic sawing motion, turning the radish with your left hand, and peeling the radish about ⅛-inch (3-mm) thick. The cutting motion should be smooth and continuous to a length of 6 to 8 inches (15 to 20 cm) at least.

5. Roll the sheets into small bundles and cut into long and thin strips.

RECTANGLES, SQUARES, AND JULIENNES

Rectangles

1. Cut the vegetable — here, the radish — at 2-inch (5-cm) intervals.

2. Trim the round sides, and shape into about 2 × 1-inch (5 × 2.5-cm) rectangular blocks.

3. Cut the blocks crosswise at even intervals depending on the thickness desired, with finger tips curved in and knuckles guiding the blade of the knife.

Squares

1. Cut the rectangular pieces in half. Or, you may halve the rectangular blocks lengthwise, and then slice the pieces crosswise at even intervals of desired thickness.

Juliennes

Stack 2 to 3 thin rectangular pieces and cut into narrow strips.

13

CUCUMBER FANS AND LEMON TWISTS

A. Cucumber Fans

1 Cut the cucumber into 1 1/2-inch (4-cm) lengths and halve the pieces lengthwise.

2 Cut out a piece of 1 × 1 1/2-inches (2.5 × 3.8-cm) and trim the flesh and seeds off.

3 Make slit cuts crosswise at about 1/8-inch (0.3-cm) intervals, leaving 1/4-inch (0.6-cm) at one end. Also, leave about 1/4-inch (0.6-cm) on both right and left ends of the piece.

4 Briefly soak in lightly salted water until pliable; fold in every other strips to form a shape of a fan.

B. Lemon Twists

Cut off a piece at about 1/3 of the length of the lemon depending on the size of the lemon. Then, cut out round pieces about 1-inch (2.5-cm) thick; cut them into 1 × 2 1/2-inch (2.5 × 6.3-cm) pieces. Remove the flesh and carefully peel off the pith underneath the skin, making the peeled surface smooth.

SINGLE STRIPS
Cut the rectangular pieces of 1 × 2 1/2-inches (2.5 × 6.3-cm) lengthwise into 2 or 3 strips.

SINGLE TWIST
1. Cut the rectangular pieces of 1 × 2 1/2-inches (2.5 × 6.3-cm) in half lengthwise. You may use wider rectangular pieces for wider twists.
2. Slit cut the halved rectangular pieces lengthwise in the middle leaving about 3/8-inch (1-cm) at one end.
3. Twist the slit cut pieces.

DOUBLE-TWIST
For fancier double-twist strips, three cuts are necessary on 1-inch (2.5-cm) wide rectangular pieces. You may use wider rectangular pieces for larger twists.
1. Make two cuts at 1/4-inch (6-mm) intervals from left to right, leaving about 3/8-inch (1-cm) at the right end. Do not cut through.
2. Make another cut in the middle from right to left, leaving about 3/8-inch (1-cm) at the left end. Do not cut through.
3. Twist the slit-cut strips and shape into a decorative form.

14

PREPARING SOUP STOCKS (出し)

In Japanese cuisine, it would not be an exaggeration to say that the success of dishes one prepares depends on the flavor and taste of the soup stock called *dashi* (出し). In general there are two kinds of *dashi*, *Dashi* #1 (一番出し) and *Dashi* #2 (二番出し). *Dashi* #1 is used for clear soups and should be thin so that the fragrance of other ingredients present in the soup can be enjoyed and also create a delicate balance with the *dashi* itself. *Dashi* #1 is preferably prepared just before use, for its delicate fragrance will be lost if prepared in advance; however, *Dashi* #1 and *Dashi* #2 when used for a seasoning base can be prepared in advance and refrigerated.

DASHI #1 (一番出し)

This soup stock is used mostly for clear soups such as scrambled-egg soup, clam soup, *tofu* and leek soup, and soup with lobster and greens.

INGREDIENTS (for 4 cups)
Dried kelp, $\frac{2}{3}$ to 1 oz (20 to 30 g)
Dried bonito shavings (*katsuobushi*), $\frac{2}{3}$ to 1 oz (20 to 30 g)

PROCEDURE
1. Wipe the dried kelp clean with a damp cloth. Add the kelp to $4\frac{1}{2}$ cups of water and bring it slowly to a boil in about 15 minutes over low heat. When the kelp rises to the surface, turn the heat off, cool, and take out the kelp. Save the kelp to use for Dashi #2.
2. Add fish shavings to the kelp stock and bring to a slow boil again. Do not allow to boil more than a few seconds. Turn the heat off. When the fish shavings have settled to the bottom of the pot, strain the liquid through a fine sieve or a strainer lined with several layers of cheesecloth. Save the fish shavings for *Dashi* #2.

15

DASHI #2 (二番出し)

A soup stock used for miso soup or as a basis in a large variety of dishes cooked with vegetables, fish, or meat.

INGREDIENTS (for 3 to 4 cups)
Dried kelp, $\frac{2}{3}$ to 1 oz (20 to 30 g)
Dried bonito shavings, 1 to $1\frac{1}{3}$ oz (30 to 40 g)

PROCEDURE
1. Wipe the kelp clean with a damp cloth. Add the kelp and fish shavings to $1\frac{1}{2}$ quarts of water and bring to a boil over medium heat. Then, lower the heat and simmer for 10 to 15 minutes or until the liquid is reduced to $\frac{2}{3}$ to $\frac{1}{2}$ of the original volume, depending on the flavor desired.
2. Cool and allow the kelp and fish shavings to settle to the bottom of the pot. Put through a strainer lined with several layers of cheesecloth.

OPTIONAL SUGGESTIONS
1. The kelp and bonito shavings saved from the *Dashi #1* preparation may be used for *Dashi #2* along with some fresh bonito shavings.
2. For *miso* soup, dried small shrimp or dried anchovies can be substituted for kelp and bonito shavings.
3. A wide variety of INSTANT *dashi* are available at Asian grocery stores.

KELP SOUP STOCK

This soup stock goes very nicely with fish or shellfish.

INGREDIENTS (for 4 cups)
Dried kelp, $\frac{2}{3}$ to 1 oz (20 to 30 g)

PROCEDURE
Wipe the kelp clean with a damp cloth. Soak the kelp in $4\frac{1}{4}$ cups of water for about 4 hours. Then heat the mixture over low heat until the kelp rises to the surface. Turn the heat off. Take out the kelp.
* You may simply soak the kelp overnight and skip the heating step.

PREPARING PICKLED VEGETABLES (漬け物)

A wide variety of vegetables can be pickled in salt, salt and rice bran, fermented bean paste (*miso*), or in a mixture of vinegar, sugar, and salt. Some pickles require several days while others can be prepared in a few hours. Commonly used vegetables include celery cabbages, radishes, cucumbers, turnips, carrots, egg plants, and ginger roots.

VINEGAR-PICKLED GINGER ROOTS

Vinegar-pickled ginger roots are quite unique and served as a garnish for *sushi*.

INGREDIENTS
Ginger roots, 1/4 lb.
Salt, 1/2 to 1 tablespoon
Vinegar sauce:
    Vinegar, 1/2 to 3/4 cup
    Sugar, 1/4 cup
    Water, 1/2 cup

PROCEDURE
1. Peel the ginger roots. Slice the roots into paper-thin pieces. Sprinkle with salt and let stand for one day. Drain the liquid.
2. Dissolve the sugar and salt in vinegar. Mix well.
3. Allow the salted ginger pieces to stand in the vinegar sauce for about 7 days. They are ready to use when they have become a light pinkish color.

*To add more color to the pickled ginger slices, you may use food coloring.
  Ginger shoots marinated in vinegar sauce make a good garnish: pour boiling water over ginger shoots and drain. Then marinade the shoots in vinegar sauce. They become reddish in 3 to 4 hours.

17

VINEGAR-PICKLED RADISHES

Many vegetables such as cucumbers, radishes, celery cabbages (Chinese cabbage), and cauliflower can be pickled in a mixture of vinegar, salt, and sugar.

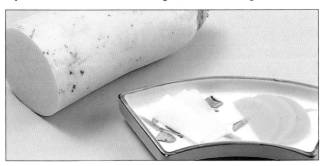

INGREDIENTS
White Japanese radishes, 1 or 2
Vinegar sauce:
    Vinegar, 1 to 1 1/4 cups
    Water, 5 cups
    Sugar, 1/2 to 3/4 cup
    Salt, 1 to 1 1/2 tablespoons
    Yellow food coloring, some (optional)

PROCEDURE
1. Peel the radishes. Cut them into 3 to 4 pieces crosswise and halve them lengthwise.
2. Pack the radishes in a crock or a glass jar and put a weight on top.
3. Combine the vinegar, water, sugar, and salt, and bring to a boil.
   Pour the hot vinegar sauce over the radishes, sufficient to cover them.
4. Keep in a cool place. It will be ready in a few days.
5. To serve, slice the radishes into half-moon shapes or rectangles.

OPTIONAL SUGGESTIONS
1. The pungent yellow Japanese radish pickle *takuan* is a favorite of many. It is pickled in salt and dry rice bran and takes several months to prepare. It is available at most Asian grocery stores.
2. Instant vinegar-pickled vegetables can be prepared by simply soaking thinly sliced vegetables in the vinegar sauce.

SALT-PICKLED CABBAGES

Just about any vegetables can be pickled with salt. The saltiness of the pickle depends on the amount of the salt sprinkled onto the vegetable.

INGREDIENTS
Celery cabbages (Chinese cabbage)
Salt

PROCEDURE
1. Trim the coarse leaves and the roots off. Cut the cabbages into 4 to 6 sections lenqth-wise and wash them. Drain the water thoroughly.
2. Sprinkle salt on each layer of the cabbage leaves. Pack the salted sections in a crock and put a weight on top (a heavy plate or a dish).
3. Put the lid on and allow to stand for 2 to 3 days.
4. To serve, rinse the pickle under running water and squeeze out the excess water. Cut into bite-size pieces.

OPTIONAL SUGGESTIONS
1. If you like the pickle a little spicy, you may tuck in several dried red peppers between the cabbage sections.
2. You may allow the pickle to ferment for a heavier taste.
3. You may prepare instant salt-pickled vegetables: cut vegetables such as carrots, radish-es, or cucumbers into thin pieces and sprinkle on salt. When the vegetable is softened, rinse the salt off, drain, and squeeze out the excess water.

PREPARING SAUCES

TERIYAKI (照燒き) SAUCE

Sweet aromatic *Teri* sauce constitutes a unique taste and also the glaze for *Teri*-dishes. *Teri* means 'gloss' in Japanese and *yaki* 'grilling.' This sauce is brushed on grilled fish, beef, pork, or chicken. It is also used as a marinating sauce.

INGREDIENTS (for ½ cup)
Soy sauce, 4 to 5 tablespoons
Sugar, 2 to 3 tablespoons
Sherry, ¼ cup
Vinegar or Lemon juice, 2 teaspoons (optional)

PROCEDURE
Combine the soy sauce, sugar, sherry, and vinegar. Bring to a boil, dissolving the sugar. Then, lower the heat and simmer for a few minutes to thicken the sauce.

TEMPURA (天ぷら) SAUCE

This simple dipping sauce enhances the delicate taste of *Tempura*.

INGREDIENTS (for 6 tablespoons)
White radish, grated, ½ cup (optional)
Ginger, grated, 2 to 3 teaspoons (optional)
Dipping sauce:
  Dashi #2 (see page 16), ¼ cup
  Soy sauce, 1 to 1 ½ tablespoons
  Sherry, 1 tablespoon
  Sugar, ½ to 1 tablespoon

PROCEDURE
1. Mix the *dashi*, soy sauce, sherry, and sugar. Heat over low heat.
2. Mix the grated radish and ginger in the hot dipping sauce just before serving. Or, make small balls of the grated radish and ginger and put in the dipping sauce.

OPTIONAL SUGGESTIONS
1. Vinegar or lemon juice may add a subtle taste to the dipping sauce.
2. *Mirin*, if available, can be substituted for sherry and sugar.

SOBA-DIPPING SAUCE

INGREDIENTS (for 3 cups)
Dashi #2, 2½ cups (see page 16)
Sherry, ¼ cup
Sugar, 2 to 3 tablespoons
Soy sauce, ¼ to ⅓ cup
Green onions, 4 to 6 stalks (coarsely chopped)
Wasabi paste, 2 to 3 tablespoons

PROCEDURE
1. Add the soy sauce, sherry, and sugar to the *dashi* and mix well, dissolving the sugar.
2. Serve with coarsely chopped green onions and *wasabi* paste.

OPTIONAL SUGGESTIONS
1. For fancier *soba*, you may serve the noodles with shredded seaweed (toasted) and bonito shavings on top.
2. *Mirin*, if available, can be substituted for sherry and sugar.

WASABI PASTE (JAPANESE GREEN MUSTARD)

Wasabi is *Wasabia japonica* in Latin and means 'mountain hollyhock' in Japanese. It is an appetizingly pungent and spicy condiment that indispensably accompanies *sashimi* as well as *sushi*.

INGREDIENTS
Wasabi powder

PROCEDURE
Mix the *Wasabi* powder with an equal volume of lukewarm water into a thick paste and allow to stand, covered, for 5 to 10 minutes. Prepare just before use.
 * Premixed *Wasabi* paste is available in tubes.

21

PREPARING FISH

DRESSING FISH

Wash the fish, here, the red snapper, in lightly salted water and place on a dampened cutting board. Dampening the cutting board prevents the fishy smell from permeating to the board and also keeps scales from sticking to it.

Scaling

Holding the head of the fish with your left hand (if right handed), scrape off the scales from the tail end, with a toothed scraper or a knife, in short strokes. Care must be taken along the belly where the flesh is soft and easily bruised. Clean thoroughly.

Gutting

Gutting methods vary depending on the shape of the fish and also depend on whether the fish is served whole. However, for fillets of round fish such as red snapper and sea bass, it is common to remove the viscera through the belly opening. Detach the bone under the jaw; insert the blade from the opening and slit open along the belly all the way down to the bottom of the stomach cage. Remove the viscera and the gills as well. Then, run the tip of the knife on the back of the stomach cage along the backbone and break the blood pockets. Wash the cavity thoroughly and pat dry.

* For narrow bodied fish such as mackerel, you may remove the head before gutting.

Removing the head

Place the fish on the cutting board, facing the back of the fish with the head on the left. Hold the head with your left hand and make a slightly diagonal cut at the base of the head, behind the gill cover. Turn the fish over and make another cut in a similar manner, removing the head.

22

FILLETING FISH

There are two common filleting techniques depending on the shape of the fish. Round fish such as red snapper, sea bass, and mackerel are generally cut into two boneless fillets, one fillet from each side of the fish, and the skeleton, thus making it a three-piece cutting (*sanmai oroshi, sanmai* meaning three pieces and *oroshi* dropping). Large fish or flat fish with wide and thin flesh, such as flounder, are cut into four fillets, two from each side of the fish, and the skeleton, thus making it a five-piece cutting (*gomai oroshi, gomai* meaning five pieces and *oroshi* dropping).

Filleting Red Snapper (Three-Piece Filleting, *Sanmai Oroshi*)

1 Rest the left hand on the fish, here, the red snapper, with the tail on the left, facing the belly. Insert the blade through the belly opening and cut open the remaining lower part down to the base of the tail.

2 Lift the partially released top layer with your left hand and insert the blade through the head opening right above the bone. Cut along the backbone, separating the flesh from the bone.

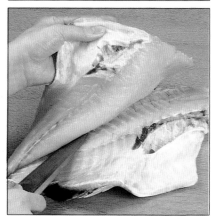

3 Continue releasing the flesh, cutting toward the back of the fish and down to the tail, leaving as little flesh as possible on the bone. Cut off the fillet at the tail base. At this point, the fish is cut in two pieces.

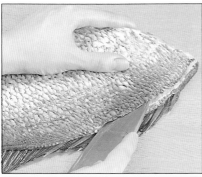

4 Turn the fish over, facing the back of the fish, with the tail on the left. Through the head opening, insert the blade near the base of the fin; slide the blade along the back and right above the backbone all the way down to the tail base, releasing the flesh.

5 Lift the partially released fillet and continue cutting toward the belly and the tail. Cut through at the base of the tail, releasing the second fillet.

6 Now the fish is in three pieces, two fillets and the skeleton.

Filleting Mackerel (Three-Piece Filleting, *Sanmai Oroshi*)

Mackerel, with a long and narrow body and thick flesh, is easier to fillet than red snapper or sea bass.

1. Place the fish on the cutting board at about a 45 degree angle facing the belly with the tail on the left. Holding the fish with your left hand (if right handed), insert the blade through the bottom of the belly opening and cut the remaining lower part all the way down to the tail.
2. Turn the fish around so that the tail is on the right and the back of the fish is in the front. Rest the left hand on the fish near the tail and make an incision on the back near the base of the tail; run the blade along the back and right above the backbone from the tail to the head end, drawing the blade toward you, releasing the fillet from the backbone. Cut through at the base of the tail. Remove the fillet. Now, the fish is cut in two pieces: a fillet and the remaining fish with the backbone.
3. Turn the fish over, putting the head-side on the right facing the back. Resting your hand lightly on the fish, slide the blade along the back and above the backbone from the head to the tail.
4. Turn the fish around, facing the belly with the tail on the right. Rest your hand lightly on the fish and insert the knife through the belly opening near the tail base; run the blade right above the backbone from the tail to the head end, detaching at the tail base.
5. Now the fish is in three pieces, two fillets and a skeleton.

Filleting Flat Fish (Five-Piece Filleting, *Gomai Oroshi*)

1. Scale the dark brown top side, the white bottom is scale free.
2. Place the fish on a dampened cutting board, facing the top side with the tail on the left. Make two angled cuts behind the gills, releasing the head. Remove the viscera and clean the cavity thoroughly. Pat dry.
3. Place the fish on the board with the head at top, facing the top side. Make an incision along the backbone down to the tail base and also make a slit-cut across the base of the tail. Do not cut through.
4. Insert the blade through the opening at the tail base and work up along the base of the fin all the way to the head opening, the edge of the blade facing the top .
5. Turn the fish around, placing the tail at the top. Holding the partially released piece, cut through at the tail base; slide the blade right above the backbone toward the fin base and the head opening, releasing the fillet.
6. In a similar fashion, release another fillet from the top side of the fish, and two fillets from the bottom side of the fish. The fish will be in five pieces, four fillets and a skeleton.

TRIMMING THE FILLETS
Red Snapper Fillets

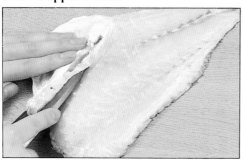

1 Removing the stomach cage. Place the fillet skin-side down, and slice off the stomach cage.
  * You may cut off the part containing the stomach cage all together: there is not much flesh that can be used for *sushi* or *sashimi.*

2 Cutting the fillets into two pieces. Cut each fillet into two pieces along the demarcation line, leaving the narrow band of bones on the belly side of the fillet.
  * If preferred, you may first cut each fillet into two pieces along the demarcation line, and then remove the stomach cage.

3 Removing the bones. Cut out the band of bones from the belly-side fillets and also pluck out any bones still remaining on the fillets with a pair of flat-bottomed tweezers.

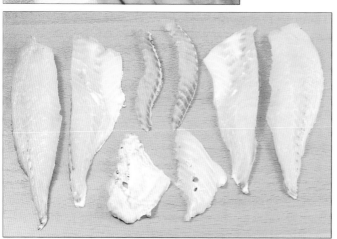

4 Fillets for *sashimi* or *nigiri-zushi.* Now, trim the fillets into four pieces which can be used for *sashimi* or *nigiri-zushi.*

SKINNING

Place the fillet, here, the red snapper, on a dampened cutting board, the skin-side down and the tail end on the left. Hold the tail end with your left hand (if right handed) and make an incision between the skin and the flesh at the near end of the fillet as possible, the blade of the knife facing the right. Pull the skin to the left, while sliding the knife to the right in a sawing motion holding the blade almost parallel to the board, skinning as close to the skin as possible.

SLICING FILLETS

Depending on the shape and the texture of the fish, fillet-slicing techniques as well as the thickness of the slices vary to bring out the best taste. Slices of soft-fleshed fish are thicker than those of the firm-fleshed.

*Getting ready — Prepare a bowl of vinegar-water (2 cups of water and 2 tablespoons of vinegar) and float a slice of lemon. Dampen a kitchen cloth and a cutting board with vinegar-water. Wipe the blade of the knife with the damp kitchen cloth. Dip your left fingers in the vinegar-water and blot off the excess water on the damp kitchen cloth.

Thin Slices (薄造り)

Firm and white-fleshed fish such as sea bass, red snapper, and halibut can be cut in thin slices.

1 Lay the fillet, here, the red snapper, on the dampened board (not wet) facing the skinned side up and the tail end to the left.

2 Place your left hand lightly on the left tip of the fillet, holding the knife almost parallel to the fillet, the edge of the blade facing to the left. Insert the blade to the fillet, slightly slanted to the right; draw the knife toward you from the base of the blade to the tip, slicing through the fillet at about $\frac{1}{16}$-inch (1.5-mm) intervals.

3 Transfer each slice immediately to serving plates and arrange in decorative patterns.

27

Flat Cuts (平造り)

This cutting method can be used for almost any fish, including those with fragile thick flesh which can be easily damaged.

1 Lay the fillet, here, the tuna block, about 2-inch (5-cm) wide and 1-inch (2.5-cm) thick, on the dampened (not wet) cutting board.

2 Place your left hand lightly on the fillet and cut the fillet straight down at ⅜-inch (1-cm) intervals into 2 × 1 × ⅜-inch (5 × 2.5 × 1-cm) rectangular pieces.

Cube Cuts (角造り)

Fish with thick and soft flesh such as tuna and yellow tail are cut into cubes.

1 Halve the rectangular pieces of 2 × 1 × ⅜ inch (5 × 2.5 × 1-cm) (see the rectangular cuts) crosswise into 1 × 1 × ⅜-inch (2.5 × 2.5 × 1-cm) cubes.

* You may first halve the rectangular block (2-inch wide and 1-inch thick) lengthwise, and then, slice the halved pieces at ½-inch (1.3-cm) intervals.

Thread Cuts (いど切り)

Long and narrow strips are prepared from very thin fillets of garfish or squid.

1 Place the fillet flat on the cutting board and draw the knife from the top to the bottom at 1/16 to ⅛-inch (1.5 to 3-mm) intervals, producing about 2- inch (5-cm) long, narrow strips.

2 Serve as a stack of strips or as a neatly arranged mound.

Ⅲ. TEN LESSONS IN JAPANESE COOKING

Lesson 1
MISO SHIRU
MISO SOUP みそ汁 (汁物)

Lesson 2
EBI SUIMONO
CLEAR SOUP WITH SHRIMP えび吸い物 (吸い物)

Lesson 3
SUNOMONO
SALAD WITH VINEGAR DRESSING 酢の物 (酢の物)

Lesson 4
CHAWANMUSHI
EGG CUSTARD IN TEA CUPS 茶碗蒸し (蒸し物)

Lesson 5
UDON
NOODLES うどん (めん類)

Lesson 6
TERIYAKI
GRILLED WITH *TERI* SAUCE 照り焼き (焼き物)

Lesson 7
TEMPURA
DEEP-FRIED SHRIMP AND VEGETABLES 天ぷら (揚げ物)

Lesson 8
SUKIYAKI
ONE-POT DISH すき焼き (鍋物)

Lesson 9
SASHIMI
SLICED RAW FISH (刺し身)

Lesson 10
SUSHI
SEASONED RICE TOPPED WITH GARNISHES (すし)

30

MISO SHIRU
MISO SOUP みそ汁
(汁物)

Miso is a thick paste of fermented soy bean. In general, white *miso* is sweet and less saltier than the red. The darker the color, the saltier the *miso*. It is quite simple to prepare *miso* soup, and yet, it is quite nutritious, rich in protein. You may create a number of variations using vegetables, shellfish, fish cake (*kamaboko*), bean curd (*tofu*), or fried bean curd (*abulahage*). On the other hand, for a simple, hurried *miso* soup, you may even leave out the bean curd which is included in this menu and just garnish with chopped green onions.

INGREDIENTS (4 servings)

Soup stock (*Dashi* #2), 3 to 3½ cups
    Dried kelp, ⅔ to 1 oz (20 to 30 g)
    Dried bonito shavings (*katsuobushi*), 1 to 1⅓ oz (30 to 40 g)
Miso paste, 2 to 3 tablespoons
Green onions, 2 to 3 stalks
Bean curd (*Tofu*), ¼ to ⅓ block
Soy sauce

PROCEDURE

1. Cut the bean curd.
2. Cut the green onions.
3. Prepare the soup stock.
4. Soften the *miso* paste.
5. Add the *miso* and bean curd to the soup stock.
6. Garnish with the green onions.

OPTIONAL SUGGESTIONS

1. Soup stock can be prepared in advance and refrigerated.
2. When dried fish shavings are not available, dried small shrimp or dried anchovies may be substituted.

1 Cutting the bean curd. Slice the bean curd crosswise at ½-inch intervals. Then cut the slices lengthwise into ½ × ½-inch (1.3 × 1.3-cm) strips. Cut the strips into ½-inch (1.3-cm) cubes.

2 Cutting the green onions. Cut the green onions into small rings.

3 Preparing the soup stock (*Dashi #2*). Wipe the kelp clean with a damp cloth. Add the kelp and fish shavings into 1 ½ quarts of water and bring to a boil. Then, simmer over low heat until the volume of the liquid is reduced to ⅔ to ½ of the original volume. Remove from the heat and allow the kelp and fish shavings to settle to the bottom of the pot. Strain through a fine sieve or a strainer lined with several layers of cheesecloth.

4 Softening the *miso* paste. Soften the *miso* paste in a small volume of soup stock, free of lumps.

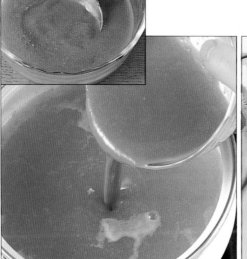

5 Adding the *miso* and bean curd. Heat the soup stock. Add the *miso* and bean curd cubes; then, swirl gently and add salt or soy sauce to taste. Bring the soup to a boil and turn the heat off. Do not allow to boil more than a few seconds once the *miso* is added. When boiled too long, it loses its flavor.

6 Garnishing. Garnish with the chopped green onions. Put the lid on immediately and serve hot.

* You may add the green onions to the soup just before turning the heat off.

EBISUIMONO

CLEAR SOUP WITH SHRIMP えび 吸い物
(吸い物)

An exquisite arrangement of pink shrimp, mushrooms, spinach, and a lemon rind in clear soup is quite impressive, appealing to the eye as well as refreshingly appetizing with a savory aromatic flavor. A large variety of vegetables and fish or shellfish may be used. It can be very elaborate with exotic ingredients such as lobsters, or it can be prepared with leftover-scraps.

INGREDIENTS (4 servings)
Soup stock (*Dashi* #1 for soup base and seasoning sauce), 4 $\frac{1}{2}$ to 5 cups
  Dried kelp, $\frac{3}{4}$ to 1 $\frac{1}{4}$ oz (25 to 38 g)
  Dried bonito shavings (*katsuobushi*), $\frac{3}{4}$ to 1 $\frac{1}{4}$ (25 to 38 g)
Shrimp (medium), 8
Spinach, $\frac{1}{4}$ to $\frac{1}{3}$ bunch
Japanese mushrooms (*Shiitake* mushrooms), 4
Fish cake, $\frac{1}{2}$ bar
Lemon rind (optional)
Soy sauce
Seasoning sauce:
  Soup stock (*Dashi* #1), 2 cups
  Soy sauce, 1 tablespoon
  Salt, dash

PROCEDURE
1. Prepare the soup stock (*Dashi* #1)
2. Prepare the shrimp, fish cake, vegetables, and lemon flowers.
3. Cook the shrimp, fish cake, and vegetables.
4. Season the soup stock.
5. Pour the soup.

OPTIONAL SUGGESTIONS
1. There is a large number of aromatic vegetables which can be used in clear soup — chrysanthemum leaves, spinach, sesame leaves, Japanese (*shiitake*) mushrooms, nettle-tree mushrooms, and more.
2. Clam soup is easy to prepare with your favorite aromatic vegetables. Simply cook the clams and garnish with vegetables (blanch if needed) just before serving.
3. When aromatic leafy vegetables are not available, green onions can be substituted. They lend a savory aromatic flavor and a refreshingly green color to the soup.
4. You may try bean curd (*tofu*) in clear soup.

1 Preparing the soup stock (*Dashi #1*). Wipe the dried kelp clean with a damp cloth. Add the kelp to 1¼ to 1⅓ quarts of water and bring slowly to a boil in about 15 minutes over low heat. When the kelp rises to the surface, turn the heat off and take the kelp out. Add the fish shavings to the kelp stock and bring to a boil again. Turn the heat off immediately. When the fish shavings have settled to the bottom of the pot, strain the mixture through a fine sieve or a strainer lined with several layers of cheesecloth. Save the kelp and fish shavings for *Dashi #2* preparation.

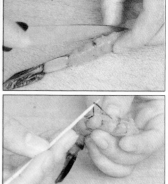

2 Preparing the shrimp, fish cake, vegetables, and lemon flowers. SHRIMP — Shell the shrimp, leaving the tails on; slit the back of the shrimp open and remove the veins. FISH CAKE — Cut the fish cake into about ¼-inch (6-mm) thick slices. MUSHROOMS — Remove the stems and make decorative cuts on the caps. SPINACH — Trim the roots and coarse leaves off. Wash the leaves and drain. LEMON FLOWERS — Cut out lemon flowers with a mold.

3 Cooking the shrimp, fish cake, and vegetables.

SHRIMP, MUSHROOMS, AND FISH CAKE — Mix the seasoning sauce and bring to a boil. Briefly cook the shrimp, fish cake, and mushrooms separately in the seasoning sauce and keep them warm. SPINACH— Bring the seasoning sauce back to a boil and blanch the spinach. Cool and squeeze out the sauce. Cut the cooked spinach into 2-inch (5-cm) lengths, if necessary.

4 Seasoning the soup stock. Heat 2½ to 3 cups of soup stock and add soy sauce and salt to taste. Bring the soup to a boil.

5 Pouring the soup. Arrange the shrimp, mushrooms, fish cake, and spinach in individual soup bowls and pour the hot soup over the ingredients. Put the lid on immediately. Serve hot.

SUNOMONO

SALAD WITH VINEGAR DRESSING 酢の物
(酢の物)

Sunomo, which means 'vinegared things,' is the Western equivalence of salad with light dressing. A large variety of aromatic vegetables as well as fish and shellfish, either raw or cooked, are delicately blended with the flavor of vinegar dressing containing vinegar, soy sauce, sherry, sugar, and toasted sesame seeds. Furthermore, strips of vinegar-pickled vegetables add a piquant taste to the salad. *Sunomono* is served in small portions and complements the main dish.

INGREDIENTS (4 servings)
Cucumbers, 1 to 2
Radish (small), ½
Red onions (small), 1 to 1 ½
Dried seaweed, 1 sheet (optional)
Vinegar-pickled carrot, ½ (optional)
Vinegar dressing :
    Vinegar, 3 to 4 tablespoons
    Sugar, 1 to 1 ½ tablespoons
    Soy sauce, 2 to 3 tablespoons
    Sherry, 2 tablespoons
    Soup stock (*Dashi* #2), 1 to 2 tablespoons (see page 16)
    Sesame seeds (toasted), 2 tablespoons
    Lemon juice, ½ tablespoon (optional)

PROCEDURE
1. Prepare the vegetables.
2. Soften the vegetables.
3. Mix the vinegar dressing.
4. Toast the seaweed.
5. Pour the dressing over the vegetables.
6. Garnish.

OPTIONAL SUGGESTIONS
1. Any fresh salad greens may be served with vinegar dressing without pretreating them with salt. If you like spicy food, you may spike the taste with black pepper and red pepper powder; a few drops of red pepper sauce will also add a tangy taste.
2. If you like chicken, you may include precooked lean chicken meat along with vegetables.

◀ **Preparing the vegetables.** RED ONIONS — Peel the onions and trim the root-base off. Half the onions lengthwise. Then put the cut surface flat on the cutting board and slice thinly into narrow half rings. CUCUMBERS — Cut the cucumbers into 2-inch (5-cm) pieces. Then, thinly slice the pieces lengthwise. Stack a couple of thin slices and julienne. RADISH — Peel the radish and cut into 2-inch (5-cm) pieces. Trim the round sides and thinly slice the pieces lengthwise. Then, stack the slices and cut into narrow strips. VINEGAR-PICKLED CARROTS (prepared in advance, see Techniques of Japanese Cooking, page 18) — Cut the thin slices of vinegar-pickled carrots into narrow strips.

2 Softening the vegetables. RADISHES AND CUCUMBERS —Sprinkle salt over the cucumber and radish strips, and allow to stand until softened. Rinse quickly, drain, and squeeze out the excess water.

3 Mixing the vinegar dressing. Mix the vinegar, sugar, soy sauce, sherry, sesame seeds, lemon juice, and soup stock together.

4 Toasting the seaweed. Toast the seaweed briefly in a heavy skillet until crisp. Do not burn. Cut the toasted seaweed into 1½-inch (4-cm) widths. Stack the sheets and cut into narrow strips.

5 Pouring the dressing. Arrange the vegetables in small individual bowls. Pour the dressing over the mixture.

6 Garnishing. Garnish with several strips of seaweed before serving.

CHAWANMUSHI

SHRIMP CUSTARD IN TEA CUPS 茶碗蒸し
(蒸し物)

Chawanmushi means 'steamed in tea cups.' This savory shrimp custard with a delicate texture and sealed-in aromatic flavor can be served as an elegant substitute for soup. It can be served either hot or cold. It is simple to prepare, and you can create your own combination of vegetables and aromatic ingredients in any heat proof cups with cover.

INGREDIENTS (4 servings)

Eggs, 3 to 4
Spinach, several leaves (small)
Fresh Japanese mushrooms (small), 1 to 2
Shrimp (small), 4
Gingko nuts, some (optional)
Carrot (small), 1/4 (optional)
Soup stock (*Dashi* #2), 2 1/2 to 3 cups:
    Dried kelp, 2/3 oz (20 g)
    Dried fish shavings (*katsuobushi*), 1/3 oz (10 g)
Soup stock seasonings:
    Soy sauce, 1 to 1 1/2 teaspoons
    Sherry, 1/2 to 1 tablespoon
    Sugar, 1/4 to 1/2 teaspoon (optional)
    Salt, dash

PROCEDURE

1. Prepare the soup stock.
2. Prepare the shrimp.
3. Prepare the vegetables.
4. Mix the custard base.
5. Fill the cups.
6. Steam the mixture.
7. Decorate with carrot flowers.
8. Serve.

OPTIONAL SUGGESTIONS

1. For an added flavor and taste, you may briefly cook the shrimp and mushrooms in a mixture of soup stock, soy sauce, sherry, and sugar.
2. You may cut the ingredients into small pieces.
3. For *chawanmushi*, there is a wide range of vegetables, nuts, and meat that can be used: bamboo shoots, parsley, watercress, green peas, celery, chestnuts, pine nuts, beef, pork, chicken, shellfish, and more.
4. In place of *Dashi* #2, you may use chicken soup stock.

1 **Preparing the soup stock.** Wipe the dried kelp clean with a damp cloth. Add the kelp and fish shavings to 4 cups of water and bring to a boil. Then simmer over low heat for about 10 minutes, or until the liquid is reduced to about 3 cups. Cool and allow the kelp and fish shavings to settle to the bottom of the pot. Strain the mixture through a strainer lined with several layers of cheesecloth. Add soy sauce, sherry, sugar, and salt to taste.

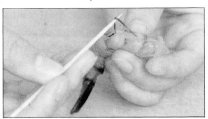

2 **Preparing the shrimp.** Clean and shell the shrimp. Slit the back of the shrimp open and remove the veins.
* You may cut them into small pieces.

3 **Preparing the vegetables.** SPINACH — Separate the leaves from the root. Wash the leaves, shake off the water, and pat dry. Cut them into 1 to 1½-inch (2.5 to 4-cm) pieces, if necessary. MUSHROOMS — Remove the stems and slice the caps thin. GINGKO NUTS — Shell and peel the nuts. CARROT FLOWERS — Stamp out thin flowers with a mold. Parboil the flowers and pat dry.

4 **Mixing the custard base.** Beat the eggs gently and mix well with the seasoned soup stock. The ratio of beaten eggs to soup stock is 1 to 3. Be careful not to make it foamy. If it is too foamy, spoon off the foam.

5 **Filling the cups.** Arrange the sliced mushrooms, spinach, gingko nuts, and shrimp in individual tea cups. Carefully ladle the custard base over the ingredients, filling the cups to about ½-inch (1.3 cm) from the top. Put the lids on the cups.

6 **Steaming the mixture.** Place the filled tea cups in the preheated steamer and steam over low heat for 15 to 20 minutes until the custard is set. LEAVE THE STEAMER LID AJAR WHILE COOKING. It will allow some steam to escape out of the steamer and thus provide good control for the steaming temperature.

7 **Decorating with carrot flowers.** When the custard is fairly well set, turn the heat off and carefully put a carrot flower on the top of the custard. Then continue steaming until the custard is well set.

8 **Serve.** Place the cup on a saucer and serve.

Lesson 5

UDON
NOODLES うどん
(めん類)

Noodle dishes are quite popular in Japan. They are served as light meals as well as between-meals snacks or late evening treats. For hurried meals, *udon* can be served by simply pouring the kelp soup stock seasoned with soy sauce over the noodles and garnishing with chopped green onions. On the other hand, *udon* can be quite elaborate with spinach, fish cake, and mushrooms and is very appealing with a delicately blended aroma. Furthermore, if *udon* is topped with a piece of shrimp *tempura*, it becomes *tempura udon*.

INGREDIENTS (4 SERVINGS)

Udon noodles, 1 pound (450 g)
Spinach, 1/3 to 1/2 bunch
Fish cake, 1/2 block (decorative fish cake, optional)
Fresh Japanese mushrooms, 4
Green onions, 3 to 4
Seaweed, 1 sheet (optional)
Soy sauce
Soup stock (for soup and seasoning sauce) 8 cups:
    Kelp, 1 to 1 1/2 oz (30 to 45 g)
    Dried bonito shavings, 1 1/2 to 2 oz (45 to 60 g)
Seasoning sauce:
    Soup stock, 1 1/2 to 2 cups
    Sherry, 2 tablespoons
    Soy sauce, 2 to 3 tablespoons
    Sugar, 2 to 3 teaspoons
    Salt, dash
Seasonings for soup:
    Soup stock, 6 cups
    Soy sauce, 3 to 3 1/2 tablespoons
    Sugar, 2 to 3 tablespoons
    Salt, dash

PROCEDURE

1. Prepare the soup stock.
2. Prepare the vegetables and fish cake.
3. Season the vegetables and fish cake.
4. Prepare seaweed strips.
5. Cook the noodles.
6. Put all the ingredients together.
7. Pour the soup.
8. Garnish.

OPTIONAL SUGGESTIONS

1. Fried bean curd strips may be added to *udon*.
2. If dried fish shavings are not available, dried small shrimp or dried anchovies may be substituted (see Techniques of Japanese Cooking, page 16).
3. For additional flavor and taste, some bonito shavings may be added on the top of the mixture along with green onions, just before serving.
4. You may use INSTANT *dashi* available at Asian grocery stores.

1 **Preparing the soup stock.** Add the kelp and fish shavings to 8½ cups of water and bring to a boil. Then lower the heat and simmer for about 10 minutes. Cool. Strain the mixture through a fine sieve or a strainer lined with several layers of cheesecloth.

2 **Preparing the vegetables and fish cake.** MUSHROOMS — Remove the stems and make decorative cuts on the caps. You may cut the caps into 3 to 4 pieces. SPINACH — Trim the roots and coarse leaves off. Wash and drain. GREEN ONIONS — Trim off the roots and coarse leaves. Wash, drain, and cut into small rings (straight cutting). FISH CAKE — Cut the fish cake into thin slices, about ⅕-inch (0.5-cm) thick.

3 **Seasoning the vegetables and fish cake.** MUSHROOMS AND FISH CAKE— Mix the seasoning sauce and bring to a boil; cook the mushrooms and fish cake briefly in the seasoning sauce. SPINACH — Bring the seasoning sauce back to a boil and parboil the spinach. Drain well and cut into 1¾-inch (4.5-cm) lengths, if necessary. Keep the cooked ingredients warm.

4 **Preparing seaweed strips.** Toast the seaweed in a heavy skillet until crisp. DO NOT BURN. Cut the toasted seaweed into about 2-inch (5-cm) widths, and then cut the pieces crosswise into narrow strips.

5 **Cooking the noodles.** Heat about 2½ quarts of water and bring to a boil. Add the noodles and stir with chopsticks to prevent the strands from sticking together and becoming lumpy. When the mixture returns to a boil, add 1 cup of water and bring to a boil again. Lower the heat and cook until the noodles have taken on a rounded shape. Take out a couple of strands, dip in cold water, and chew it. It should have body to it and still be chewy. DO NOT OVERCOOK. Turn the heat off. Immediately rinse with cold water and drain.

6 **Putting all the ingredients together.** Divide the noodles into four portions and put them in deep soup bowls. On the top of the noodles, neatly arrange the cooked fish cake, mushrooms, and spinach.

7 **Pouring the soup.** Season the soup stock with the soy sauce, sugar, and salt. Bring to a boil. Then, pour the hot soup over the mixture.

8 **Garnishing.** Add the chopped green onions and seaweed strips on the top of the *udon.* Serve immediately.

TERIYAKI
SALMON *TERIYAKI* · BEEF *TERIYAKI*
GRILLED WITH TERI SAUCE 照り焼き
(焼き物)

Many Westerners are quite familiar with Beef *Teriyaki*, beef grilled with *Teri* sauce. *Teri* means 'gloss' and *yaki* 'grilling.' *Teri* sauce is a mixture of three basic ingredients, that is, soy sauce, sherry, and sugar; it glazes the food when cooked. A large variety of food can be grilled with *teri* sauce — beef, chicken, fish, and shellfish as well as some vegetables such as mushrooms, carrots, and bell peppers. Fish *teriyaki* is also popular in Japan.

A. SALMON *TERIYAKI* (さけの 照り燒き)

It is quite common to serve fish *teriyaki* with vinegar-pickled shallots (*rakkyo*), or vinegar-marinated ginger shoots known as 'bashful ginger (*hajikami shoga*).' You can also add toasted gingko nuts and chestnuts.

INGREDIENTS (4 servings)

Salmon, 4 pieces
Teri Sauce:
    Soy sauce, 4 to 5 tablespoons
    Sherry, ¼ cup
    Sugar, 2 to 3 tablespoons (or *mirin*, 3 to 4 tablespoons)
    Vinegar or lemon juice, 2 teaspoons (optional)
Gingko nuts, some (optional)
Chestnuts, some (optional)
Vinegar-marinated ginger shoots, 4 (optional)

PROCEDURE

1. Prepar-pickled the *teri* sauce.
2. Cook the fish.
3. Baste the fish with *teri* sauce.
4. Serve.

OPTIONAL SUGGESTIONS

Vinegar-pickled vegetables such as radishes, carrots, or even cauliflower lend a refreshing compliment to the grilled fish. They are easily prepared by simply soaking small pieces of them in vinegar sauce. Allow to stand until the vegetables have absorbed the taste of vinegar and sugar (see Techniques of Japaness Cooking, page 18).

Preparing the *teri* sauce. Mix the soy sauce, sherry, sugar, and lemon juice and simmer for a few minutes to thicken the sauce.

2 **Cooking the fish.** Grill over medium heat, skin side down, until light brown. Sprinkle with a dash of salt, if desired. Turn over. Lower the heat and continue cooking until light brown, about 90% cooked.

3 **Basting the fish with *teri* sauce.** Brush on or spoon the *teri* sauce over the fish and cook briefly; repeat this step once more. DO NOT BURN. Just before removing the fish from the grill, brush on the sauce one more time. When the sauce is cooled, the fish pieces will take on a glossy look.

4 **Serving.** Serve the grilled fish with toasted gingko nuts, toasted chestnuts, and vinegar-marinated ginger shoots (see Techniques of Japanese Cooking, page 17), if available.

B. BEEF *TERIYAKI* (牛肉 照り焼き)

This beef dish is a favorite of many Westerners. Just imagine the dripping of the *teri* sauce and meat fat over a red hot charcoal spitting off an exotic aroma. Vegetables such as bell peppers and mushrooms grilled along with the beef is an excellent accompaniment to beef *teriyaki:* the aroma of the vegetables blended with *teriyaki* beef further sharpens the appetite.

INGREDIENTS (4 servings)

Tender beef loin, ½ lb (230 g)
Fresh Japanese mushrooms (med), 4 to 6
Bell peppers (med), 2
Carrot, ⅓ to ½ (optional)
Teri Sauce:
  Soy sauce, 4 to 5 tablespoons
  Sherry, ¼ cup
  Sugar, 2 to 3 tablespoons

PROCEDURE

1. **Prepare the beef.** Cut the beef into pieces about ½-inch (1.5-cm) thick and 1½-inch (4-cm) wide. Then cut the pieces crosswise at ¾ to 1-inch (2 to 2.5-cm) intervals against the grain.

2. **Prepare the vegetables.** MUSHROOMS — Remove the stems, and cut the caps in half. BELL PEPPERS — Quarter the peppers lengthwise, seed, and remove the pith. Slice the quartered pieces crosswise. CARROT (optional) — Peel the carrot and wedge-cut it into small pieces; soak them in vinegar sauce. Allow to stand until the carrots taste appetizingly sour and sweet. Should be prepared in advance. (See Techniques of Japanese Cooking, page 18.)

3. **Mix the *teri* sauce.** Combine the soy sauce, sherry, and sugar. Bring to a boil. Then, lower the heat and simmer to thicken the sauce and bring out the sheen.

4. **Grill and baste the beef and vegetables with *teri* sauce.** Arrange the beef and vegetables on skewers and cook at medium heat until almost cooked the way you like to have your steaks done. Brush the *teri* sauce over the food and cook briefly; repeat this step one more time. Then, just before taking them out from the grill, brush the sauce over the meat and vegetables. When the sauce is cooled, the meat and vegetables will look appetizingly glossy. DO NOT OVER COOK. Beef *teriyaki* tastes best when succulent.

5. **Serve.** Serve the grilled beef and vegetables on or off the skewers, and you may add the vinegar-pickled carrots.

OPTIONAL SUGGESTIONS

1. Onions, bell peppers, or mushrooms can be pan-fried with *teri* sauce and served as a side dish with beef *teriyaki.*
2. As with fish *teriyaki*, vinegar-pickled vegetables (see Techniques of Japanese Cooking, page 18) lend a refreshing compliment to the beef *teriyaki.*

Lesson 7

TEMPURA
DEEP-FRIED SHRIMP AND VEGETABLES 天ぷら
(揚げ物)

Tempura, which supposedly originated by Portuguese who lived in Japan centuries ago, has become quite popular in Japanese kitchens. Crisp deep-fried shrimp is everyone's delight. Almost any vegetables such as mushrooms, sweet potatoes, onions, and carrots can be transformed into delicious *tempura*. The secret of delicately crisp *tempura* is in the batter mix and the cooking temperature. At a moderately high temperature, the surface of the food gets cooked immediately so that the food does not get greasy, and the food inside is juicy and tender and its flavor is retained. The aromatic flavor of the soft pink shrimp or the green vegetables under deliciously golden crisp coating is very inviting. Perfect for special occasions.

INGREDIENTS (4 servings)

Shrimp (med) 12 to 14
Carrot (med), 1
Sweet potato (med), 1
Bell peppers, 1 to 2
Lotus root (med), $\frac{1}{4}$
Cooking oil, 4 to 6 cups
Batter:
    Flour, 1 to 1$\frac{1}{2}$ cup
    Eggs (yolk), 1 to 2
    Water, $\frac{3}{4}$ to 1$\frac{1}{4}$ cup
Dipping sauce:
    Soup stock (*Dash* #2), $\frac{1}{4}$ cup (see page 16)
    Soy sauce, 1 to 1$\frac{1}{2}$ tablespoons
    Sherry, 1 tablespoon
    Sugar, $\frac{1}{2}$ to 1 tablespoon
    White radish, grated, $\frac{1}{4}$ cup (optional)

PROCEDURE

1. Prepare the vegetables.
2. Prepare the shrimp.
3. Mix the batter.
4. Deep-fry the vegetables and shrimp.
5. Mix the dipping sauce.
6. Serve.

OPTIONAL SUGGESTIONS

1. When deep-frying sesame leaves, garland chrysanthemum leaves, or chrysanthemum flowers, coat the under-sides with batter.
2. When deep-frying fish or vegetables high in water content, dredge them first with flour or cornstarch, and then dip in batter for crisp *tempura*.
3. For crispier *tempura*, cornstarch and baking powder may be added to the batter.
4. If you do not have an electric frying pot, a wok is the second choice for deep-frying. Because of the shape of the wok, less oil is needed than when using a flat bottomed pot and the heat is evenly distributed giving even temperature control to the oil.

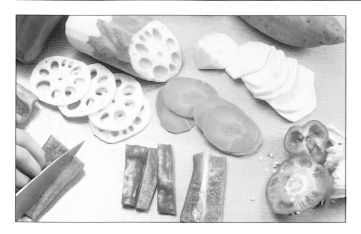

1 **Preparing the vegetables.** CARROT — Cut the carrot into thin round slices. BELL PEPPERS — Halve the bell peppers lengthwise and remove the pith and seeds. Cut the pieces into 2 to 3 slices lengthwise. SWEET POTATO— Cut the sweet potato in thin, round pieces. LOTUS ROOT— Peel the root and cut into thin round slices. To prevent discoloration, soak the sweet potato and lotus root slices in a slightly acidic solution (1 tablespoon of vinegar or lemon juice in 2 cups of water) until needed. Take them out, drain well, and blot off the remaining water.

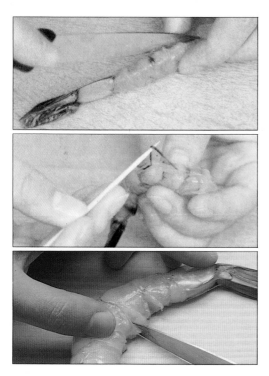

2 **Preparing the shrimp.** Shell the shrimp, leaving the tails on; blot dry the tails. Slit the back of the shrimp open and remove the veins. Make a couple of slashes across the belly to prevent the shrimp from curling during frying. DO NOT CUT THROUGH.

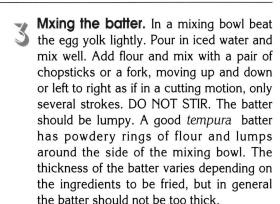

3 **Mxing the batter.** In a mixing bowl beat the egg yolk lightly. Pour in iced water and mix well. Add flour and mix with a pair of chopsticks or a fork, moving up and down or left to right as if in a cutting motion, only several strokes. DO NOT STIR. The batter should be lumpy. A good *tempura* batter has powdery rings of flour and lumps around the side of the mixing bowl. The thickness of the batter varies depending on the ingredients to be fried, but in general the batter should not be too thick.

4 **Deep-frying the vegetables and shrimp.** Heat 3 to 4 cups of oil, at least 2-inch (5-cm) deep, to about 350° F (180° C) over medium heat. When a drop of the batter does not go all the way down to the bottom and starts rising from mid way, the oil is ready for frying. FRYING THE VEGETABLES — Dredge the vegetable slices with flour, dust off the excess flour, and dip in the batter. Put them carefully in the oil, one by one. DO NOT CARRY EXCESS BATTER TO THE OIL to avoid making the *tempura* too lumpy. If necessary, occasionally strain out batter spatterings so that the fried pieces look clean, free of burned debris. Do not add too many pieces at one time: the oil temperature should be fairly well maintained through out the course of frying. When the pieces have risen to the surface sizzling, turn them over and cook for a few seconds or longer, depending on the thickness of the vegetable pieces, until golden brown. DO NOT BURN. Take them out using a strainer or a pair of chopsticks. Drain. FRYING THE SHRIMP — Dredge the shrimp with flour and dust off the excess flour. Dip in the batter holding by the tail, then carefully put in the heated oil. When the shrimp have come up to the surface, turn them over and cook for a few seconds, until golden brown. Take them out and drain.

5 **Mixing the dipping sauce.** Combine the soup stock (*Dashi* #2), soy sauce, sherry, and sugar. Heat and mix well. Pour the hot dipping sauce into individual sauce bowls and put a dab of the grated radish and ginger in each bowl.

 *You may make small balls of the grated radish and ginger and put in the individual sauce bowls containing the dipping sauce.

6 **Serving.** Serve the *tempura* with the dipping sauce. For a simple dipping sauce, you may leave out the grated radish and ginger.

SUKIYAKI

ONE-POT DISH すき焼き
(鍋物)

Sukiyaki cooked in a shallow pot at the dinner table appeals to everyone's palate. The word *sukiyaki* means 'thinly sliced and roasted' in Japanese. Its origin seems to date back to when farmers in the field used to roast meat of wild game over an open fire. The ingredients and seasoning sauce used are quite elementary; yet, as it cooks, the seasoning sauce seeps into the meat and vegetables which in turn lend unique flavors, creating an exquisite taste. No two hostesses can ever prepare *Sukiyaki* exactly the same even with an identical recipe. Furthermore, you may create as many variations as your fancy allows. In general, there are Tokyo style and Osaka style *sukiyaki*. The Tokyo style *sukiyaki* is prepared leisurely, cooking the meat separately before adding the vegetables, while the Osaka style *sukiyaki* is prepared all together, that is, all the ingredients including the beef are beautiful-ly arranged in the pot beforehand and brought to the table: beef and vegetables are cooked together. Customarily, a whipped egg is served in each individual bowl. The cooked food is dipped in the whipped egg, the hot food cooking the egg upon contact and thus being thinly coated with the egg which tenderizes the bite of the food.

INGREDIENTS (4 servings)
Sirloin, 1 ½ pounds (680 g)
Green onions, 4 to 6
Fresh mushrooms, 8 to 10
Garland chrysanthemum leaves, ½ to 1 bunch
Celery cabbage, ¼
Fish cake (*kamaboko*), 1 to 1 ½ blocks (optional)
Devil's tongue jelly (*konnyaku*), ½ to 1 block (optional)
Bean curd (*Tofu*), ½ block
Seasoning sauce:
    Soup stock (*Dashi* #2), 2 ½ to 3 cups (see page 16)
    Soy sauce, ¼ to ½ cup
    Sherry, ¼ to ½ cup
    Sugar, ¼ to ½ cup
    Salt

PROCEDURE
1. Prepare the meat.
2. Prepare the vegetables, bean curd, and devil's tongue jelly.
3. Mix the seasoning sauce.
4. Arrange the meat, vegetables, bean curd, and devil's tongue jelly in the pot.
5. Add the seasoning sauce and cook.
6. Serve.

OPTIONAL SUGGESTIONS
1. Spinach may be substituted for garland chrysanthemum leaves.
2. Dried mushrooms (softened) may be used in place of fresh mushrooms.
3. Gelatinous noodles cooked along with meat and vegetables offer another unique variation.
4. You may cook the meat first in the oiled pot, then add the vegetables and seasoning sauce and continue cooking.
    ＊For traditional Japanese *sukiyaki*, beef suet is used.
5. You may serve whipped eggs with *sukiyaki*.

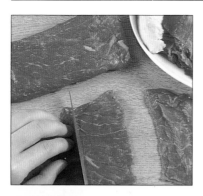

1 **Preparing the meat.** Have the beef cut into thin sheets, preferably paper thin. Cut the thin sheets against the grain into 2 × 2½-inch (5 × 6-cm) pieces.

2 **Preparing the vegetables, bean curd, and devil's tongue jelly.** GREEN ONIONS — Trim the roots and coarse leaves off, wash, and drain. Cut them into diagonal pieces, about 2-inch (5-cm) long. MUSH-ROOMS — Wash the mushrooms and remove the stems. Make decorative cuts on the caps. GARLAND CHRYSANTHEMUM LEAVES — Trim off the roots and coarse leaves. Wash and drain. Cut them into 2½-inch (6-cm) lengths, if necessary. CABBAGE — Separate the cabbage leaves and trim the coarse tips off. Wash the leaves and drain. Halve the leaves lengthwise, then cut the pieces crosswise into about 1¼-inch (3.2-cm) lengths. DEVIL'S TONGUE JELLY — Cut the devil's tongue jelly into 1½ × ¾ × ¼-inch (3.8 × 1.9 × 0.6-cm) pieces. BEAN CURD — Slice the bean curd into 1½ × ¾ × ½-inch (3.8 × 1.9 × 1.3-cm) pieces.

3 **Mixing the season-ing sauce.** Combine the soup stock, soy sauce, sherry, and sugar. Add salt to taste. Warm the mix-ture and dissolve the sugar and salt. Mix well.

4 **Arranging the meat, vegetables, bean curd, and devil's tongue jelly in the pot.** Neatly arrange about one third of the ingredients in the pot.
  * You may add the garland chrysanthemum leaves when the rest of the ingredients are almost cooked. (They cook quite rapidly.)

5 **Adding the seasoning sauce and cooking.** Pour about one-third of the seasoning sauce over the mixture and bring to a boil. Lower the heat and continue cooking. Once served, replenish the pot: add another batch of the ingredients and the seasoning sauce as necessary.

6 **Serving.** Guests help themselves to the *sukiyaki*. Serve with rice and pickled vegetables.

SASHIMI

TUNA *SASHIMI* · RED SNAPPER *SASHIMI*

SLICED RAW FISH

(刺し身)

Sashimi is fresh raw fish slices usually served on a bed of shredded radishes along with *wasabi* (Japanese mustard), pickled ginger slivers, and soy sauce. Preparing *sashimi*, that is, slicing the fillet of raw fish or shellfish and arranging the slices with garnish is an art itself acquired through practice. There are four different ways of slicing fillets — flat cuts (平造り), cube cuts (角造り), thin slices (薄造り), and thread cuts (いど切り). The long standing Japanese tradition commands particular slicing techniques for certain fish to produce the best effect on the taste buds.

71

INGREDIENTS (4 servings)

Fish fillets, tuna and red snapper, 1 to 2 each
Wasabi powder, 4 teaspoons or premixed paste in tubes.
Vinegar-pickled ginger slivers, some (optional)
Soy sauce
Vinegar-water for finger dipping
    Vinegar, 2 tablespoons
    Water, 2 cups
    Lemon slice, 1 (optional)

PROCEDURE

1. Prepare the *wasabi* paste.
2. Slice the fillets.
3. Serve.

OPTIONAL SUGGESTIONS

You may serve the *sashimi* on a bed of shredded lettuce or long thin strips of white radish.

1 Preparing the *wasabi* paste.
Mix the *wasabi* powder with an equal volume of lukewarm water and allow to stand, covered, for about 10 minutes.

2 Slicing the fillets. GETTING READY — Prepare a bowl of vinegar-water and float a slice of lemon. Dampen a kitchen cloth and a cutting board with vinegar-water. Wipe the blade of the knife with the damp kitchen cloth. Dip your left fingers in vinegar-water and blot off the excess water on the damp kitchen cloth. RED SNAPPER FILLETS — Place the skinned fillet on the cutting board, the skinned side facing up and the tail-side on the left. Rest your left hand lightly on the fillet and slice the fillet at ⅜-inch (1-cm) intervals, by drawing the knife toward you from the base of the blade to the tip. The knife should be cleaned frequently with vinegar-water. TUNA FILLETS, rectangular blocks, 2 × 1 × 8 inch (5 × 2.5 × 20 cm) — Slice the fillet at ¼ to ⅜-inch (0.6 to 1-cm) intervals into rectangular pieces.

3 Serving. Serve the *sashimi* with soy sauce, *wasabi*, and vinegar-pickled ginger slivers.

SUSHI
NIGIRI-ZUSHI
NORI-MAKI · GUNKAN-MAKI
SEASONED RICE TOPPED WITH GARNISHES
（すし）

Sushi is vinegar-and-sugar seasoned rice topped or wrapped with garnishes such as raw fish or vegetables. Among several varieties of *sushi*, *nigiri-zushi* and *maki-zushi* are quite popular in Western countries. *Nigiri* means 'squeezing.' Thus *nigiri-zushi* (finger rolled *sushi*) is prepared by making a small oval pad of *sushi* rice and pressing it onto a piece of fish or shell fish. *Maki-zushi* (rolled *sushi*) is prepared, as the name itself implies, by rolling the *sushi* rice on a sheet of seaweed with vegetables, meat, fish, or just about any edible ingredients. *Maki-zushi* includes single-filling and multi-filling *nori-maki* (mat-rolled *sushi*), *te-maki* (hand-rolled *sushi*) which looks like an ice cream cone, and *gunkan-maki* (battle-ship-shaped *sushi*). *Gunkan-maki* is loaded much of the time with fish roe and thus gives the nick name 'roe *sushi*.' When *sushi* rice is served in a large bowl with shredded vegetables and raw fish topped with strips of thin omelette, it is called *chirashi-zushi*. This means that all the ingredients are mixed and scattered. It is fun to make *sushi*. Create your fancies with your favorite ingredients.

A. *NIGIRI-ZUSHI* (にぎりずし **FINGER ROLLED** *SUSHI*)

INGREDIENTS (4 servings, 2-dozen pieces)
Rice (short grain, uncooked), 2 cups
Seasoning sauce for *sushi* rice:
 Sugar, 2 tablespoons
 Salt, ⅛ teaspoon
 Vinegar, 2 tablespoons
Wasabi powder, 1 tablespoon
Red snapper fillets, 1 to 1 ½ pieces
Tuna fillet, 2 × 1 × 8-inch (5 × 2.5 × 20 cm), 1 block
Ginger slices, vinegar-pickled (optional)
Vinegar-water for finger dipping:
 Vinegar, 2 tablespoons
 Water, 2 cups
 Lemon slice, 1 (optional)

PROCEDURE
1. Cook the rice.
2. Mix the seasoning sauce.
3. Season the rice.
4. Make the *wasabi* paste.
5. Slice the fillets.
6. Make the *sushi.*
7. Serve the *sushi.*

OPTIONAL SUGGESTIONS
1. If you do not care for seafood, you may try smoked meat or vegetables. You can create a large variety of *nigiri-zushi* with your favorite food. The only requirement is that the food should be able to stay on the rice pad. If necessary, the food can be secured onto the rice pad by a strip of toasted seaweed.
2. Shrimp used for *sushi* topping should be cooked on skewers to prevent them from curling.

Cooking the rice. Wash the rice thoroughly until the rinsed water comes out clear. The volume of the water may vary depending on the dryness of the rice: in general 1 to 1 ¹/₁₀ times the volume of the rice is needed. Allow to stand for about 15 minutes or until well soaked. In a pot with a tight-fitting lid, bring the rice to a boil over medium heat. Then lower the heat so that the water does not spill over; continue cooking for 2 to 5 minutes. When all the water has been absorbed, still lower the heat to minimum, and cook for another 10 minutes or longer. *Sushi* rice should not be mushy. You may need to experiment to find the right condition. Turn the heat off and allow to stand for 5 to 10 minutes.

2 **Mixing the seasoning sauce.** Combine the sugar, salt, and vinegar. Mix well, dissolving the sugar and salt.

3 **Seasoning the rice.** Transfer the rice into a non-metallic container, preferably a wood container. Spread the rice with a rice paddle (or a wooden spatula) by running the paddle right to left as if in a cutting motion and turning over repeatedly. Pour the seasoning sauce over the rice a little at a time, separating the grains and cooling the rice with a paper fan. The rice should be evenly seasoned.

4 **Making the *wasabi* paste.** Mix 1 tablespoon of *wasabi* powder with an equal volume of lukewarm water, firmly thick but not lumpy. Allow this to stand, covered, for 5 to 10 minutes to absorb the spicy flavor.

5 **Slicing the fillets (Thin slices).** GETTING READY — Prepare a bowl of vinegar-water and float a slice of lemon. Dampen a kitchen cloth and a cutting board with vinegar-water. Wipe the blade of the knife with the damp kitchen cloth. Dip your left fingers in the vinegar-water and blot off the excess water on the damp kitchen cloth. SLICING THE TUNA — Place the tuna fillet on the cutting board. Rest your left hand lightly on the tip of the fillet at left; insert the cutting edge of the blade to the fillet from right to left, slightly slanted to the right (incision angle determines the width of the slices), slicing the fillet by drawing the knife toward you from the base of the blade to the tip. Cut off the first piece and continue slicing the fillet at ⅛ to ¼ inch (0.3 to 0.6-cm) intervals into about 1¼-inch (3-cm) widths, producing 2 × 1¼-inch (5 × 3-cm) pieces. The knife should be cleaned frequently. SLICING THE RED SNAPPER — Place the fillet on the board, skinned side up and the tail end on your left. Rest the left hand on the edge of the fillet at left and insert the blade of the knife from right to left to the fillet, slightly slanted to the right; slice the fillet at ⅛ to ¼-inch (0.3 to 0.6-cm) intervals into about 1¼ inch (3-cm) widths.

Making the *sushi*. GETTING READY — Dip your fingers (both hands) in the vinegar-water and remove the excess water by touching the damp kitchen cloth (if hands are too wet, the rice does not stick).

(1) PICKING UP A *SUSHI* TOPPING — Pick up a piece of tuna with the left hand and put it inside the hand.

(2) MAKING A RICE PAD — Pick up a heaping tablespoon of rice with the right hand and round it to an oval shape.

(3) SMEARING THE *WASABI* — Holding the rice in the palm of your right hand, pick up a dab of *wasabi* with your right index finger; smear on the center of the tuna.

(4) PUTTING TOGETHER — Put the rice pad on the tuna and press lightly with the left thumb.

(5) FORMING A SHAPE — With the left thumb on the side of the rice pad, curl the fingers around the rice; press down the rice pad lightly with the first two fingers of the right hand, forming a rectangular shape. GIVING A FINAL TOUCH — Roll the *sushi* from the cup of your hand to the fingers, bringing the tuna on top. Give a final squeeze on the side and even up the shape.

7 **Serving the *sushi*.** Wipe a platter with the damp kitchen cloth. Arrange the *sushi* neatly on the platter along with a mound of pickled ginger slivers. Serve with soy sauce in small individual bowls.

B. *NORI-MAKI* (のり巻 MAT-ROLLED *SUSHI*)

INGREDIENTS (4 servings)
Sheet seaweed, 8 × 10 inch (20 × 25 cm), 4 sheets
Sushi rice, 4 cups (see *nigiri zushi*)
Fillings
    Eggs, 2 to 3
    Carrot (large), 1
    Cucumber (large), 1
    Fish crumbs (fish *oboro*), some (optional)
Carrot seasoning sauce:
    Kelp soup stock, 1 ½ cups (see page 16)
    Sugar, ½ to 1 tablespoon
    Soy sauce, ½ to 1 tablespoon
    Salt, dash
Vinegar-water for finger dipping:
    Vinegar, 2 tablespoons
    Water, 2 cups

PROCEDURE
1. Prepare the vegetables.
2. Prepare the egg strips.
3. Toast the seaweed.
4. Roll the *sushi.*
5. Cut the *sushi* rolls.

OPTIONAL SUGGESTIONS
1. If preferred, use uncooked carrot strips. They are fresh and crunchy.
2. Dried gourd may be added to the above recipe, if available.
3. Thick egg strips may be used instead of the thin strips used in this recipe.

1 **Preparing the vegetables.** CARROT — Cut the carrot into about 4-inch (10-cm) lengths. Trim the round sides off and shape into rectangular blocks. Slice the rectangular blocks lengthwise into ⅜-inch (1-cm) thick pieces, then cut the pieces lengthwise at ⅜-inch (1 cm) intervals into strips. Bring the seasoning sauce to a boil and cook the carrots briefly. Drain and cool. CUCUMBER — Quarter the cucumber lengthwise into long strips.

2 **Preparing the egg strips.** Beat the eggs with a dash of salt and 1 teaspoon of sugar. Oil the frying pan thoroughly with vegetable oil and heat over low heat; wipe off the excess oil with paper towels. When a drop of the egg mixture sizzles immediately upon touching the pan, the pan is ready. Spread the egg evenly around the pan and fry briefly until all the liquid is set. Turn the heat off. Carefully take out the egg sheet and cool. Cut the sheet crosswise at ½-inch (1.3-cm) intervals.

3 **Toasting the seaweed.** Toast the seaweed in a heavy skillet until the color has turned greenish. Do not burn.

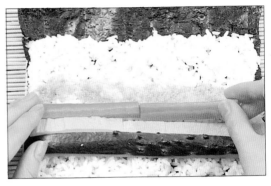

Rolling the *sushi*.

(1) SPREADING THE RICE ON THE SEAWEED — Place the *sushi* mat in front of you in such a way that it rolls away from you, not from side to side. Place a sheet of toasted seaweed on the mat, the shiny side down. Dip your fingers (both hands) in the vinegar-water and blot off the excess water on a damp kitchen cloth (dampened with vinegar-water). Then evenly spread 5 to 6 heaping tablespoons of *sushi* rice (about 1 cupful) on the seaweed, leaving about ½-inch (1.5-cm) margin at the far end.

(2) PUTTING ON THE FILLINGS — Put the carrot and cucumber strips in the middle of the rice, pressing down lightly; put on the egg strips. Then, spread a thin layer of fish crumbs.

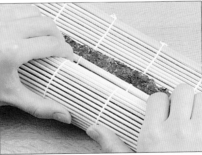

(3) ROLLING THE *SUSHI*. — Lift the *sushi* mat with both hands, placing the thumbs underneath the mat and fingers pressing down on the fillings lightly. Roll the mat, bringing the near end of the rice to the far end of the rice. Then, lift the end of the mat slightly and complete rolling, sealing the roll. Finally, compress the roll lightly across the mat, and push in the loose ends.

Cutting the *sushi* rolls. Place the *sushi* roll on the cutting board, the seam side down. Wet the blade of the knife with vinegar-water and blot off the excess water on the damp kitchen cloth. Slice the roll in half by pressing down the blade lightly from above the roll, drawing the knife toward you from the base of the blade to the tip. Slice each half into 3 to 4 pieces. Clean the knife frequently with vinegar-water.

C. *GUNKAN-MAKI* (軍艦巻 BATTLESHIP- SHAPED *SUSHI*)

INGREDIENTS (8 pieces)
Seaweed, 1 ½ × 6-inches (3.8 × 15-cm), 8 strips
Sushi rice (see *nigiri-zushi*), 8 heaping tablespoons
Fish roe, salmon and sea urchin, each 3 to 4 tablespoons
Wasabi powder, 1 teaspoon
Vinegar-water for finger dipping:
    Vinegar, 2 tablespoons
    Water, 2 cups

PROCEDURE
1. Make ships.
2. Smear the *wasabi*.
3. Fill the ships.

OPTIONAL SUGGESTIONS
1. You may fill the ships with baby scallops, clams, lobsters, or shrimp cooked, spiced, and cut into small pieces.

1. **Making ships.** GETTING READY — Prepare a bowl of vinegar-water. Dampen a kitchen cloth with vinegar-water. Dip your fingers (both hands) in the vinegar-water and blot off the excess water on the damp kitchen cloth. MAKING SHIPS — Pick up a heaping tablespoon of rice and mold into an oval shape, squeezing lightly. Wrap the *sushi* rice with a seaweed strip. Crush a couple of grains of rice on the loose end of the strip and seal the ship. The ship should be about two thirds filled with rice.

2. **Smearing the *wasabi*.** Smear a streak of *wasabi* on the rice.

3. **Filling the ships.** Fill the ships with fish roe. You may decorate the ships with cucumber fans or with any edible green leaves.

INDEX